READING FUN

Pictures by Ellen Appleby and Karen Pellaton

GOLDEN PRESS® NEW YORK
Western Publishing Company, Inc.
Racine, Wisconsin

GOLDEN FUN AT HOME WORKBOOKS

ISBN 0-307-01437-1
BCDEFGHIJ

Ready To Read

You see words every day.
At home.
In the street.
In stores.
On TV.
Outside,
inside,
everywhere.
You know many words.
Now get ready to read them.
Start on the next page.
Have fun!

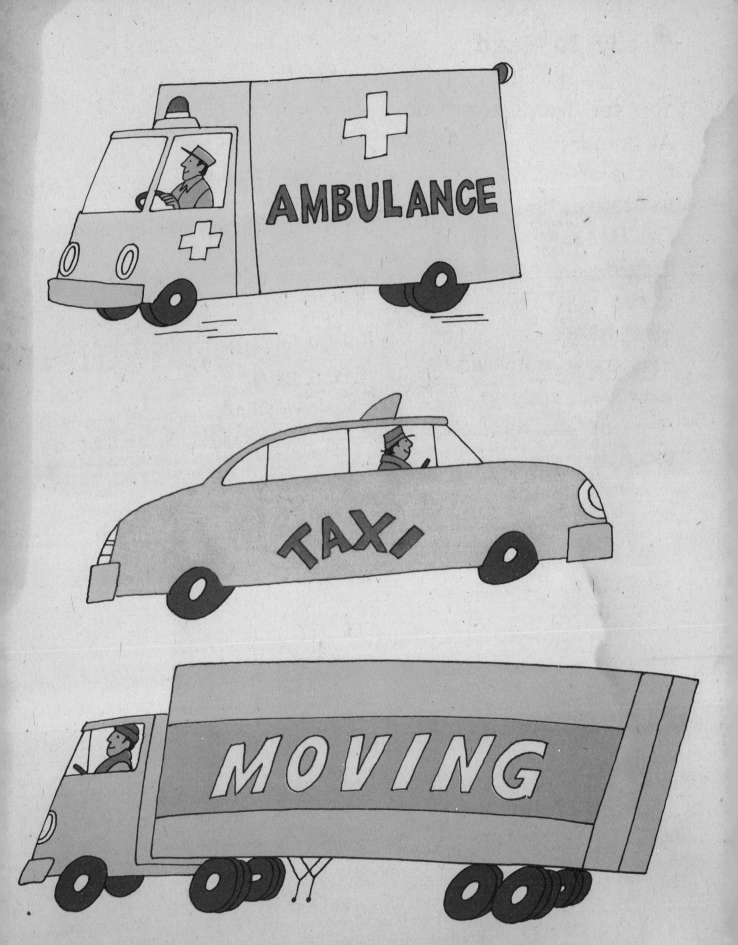

Food Words

Street Words

NO PARKING

SLOW

WALK

STOP

BUS STOP

Words for Doors

Warning Words

More Warning Words

Information Words

Direction Words

GO LEFT

GO RIGHT

UP

DOWN

What do you like on the menu?

MENU

Appetizers
Chicken Soup with Rice
Celery and Olives

Sandwiches
Grilled Cheese
Tuna Fish
Peanut Butter and Jelly

Drinks
Grape Juice
Milk

Dessert
Chocolate Chip Cookies
Apple Slices with Honey
Pudding

Read the words.
Say them out loud.
Ask for help if you need it.

taxi

ambulance

police

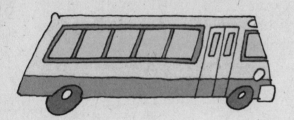

bus

walk

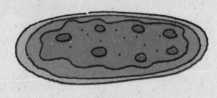

pizza

stop

women

men

Read the words.
Say them out loud.

push

pull

in

out

open

closed

hot

cold

danger

trash

Read the words.
Say them out loud.

up

down

left

right

bicycle

tree

pet

cheese

soup

milk

jelly

Here are all the letters
in the alphabet.
Say their names out loud.

Aa Bb Cc

Dd Ee

Ff Gg Hh

Ii Jj Kk

Ll Mm Nn

Oo Pp

Qq Rr Ss

Tt Uu

Vv Ww Xx

Yy Zz

Say the name
of the letter.
Then say the word out loud.

Aa   ant

Bb   bird

Cc   cat

Dd   dog

Ee   egg

Say the name
of the letter.
Then say the word out loud.

Ff  fish

Gg girl

Hh house

Ii iceberg

Jj jeans

Say the name
of the letter.
Then say the word out loud.

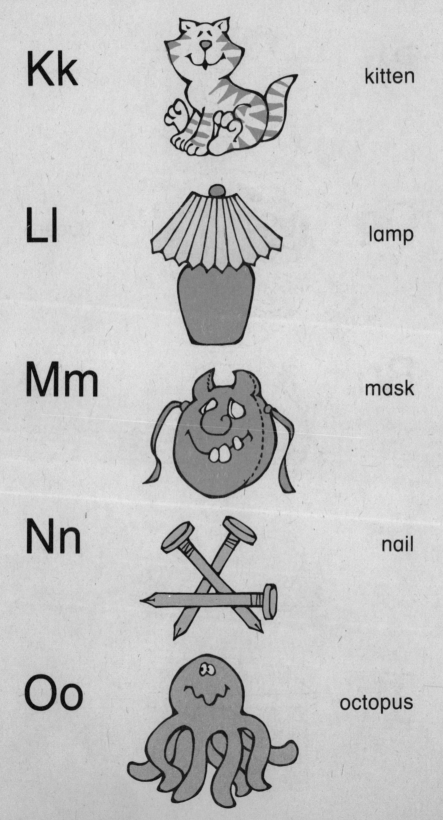

Kk   kitten

Ll   lamp

Mm   mask

Nn   nail

Oo   octopus

Say the name
of the letter.
Then say the word out loud.

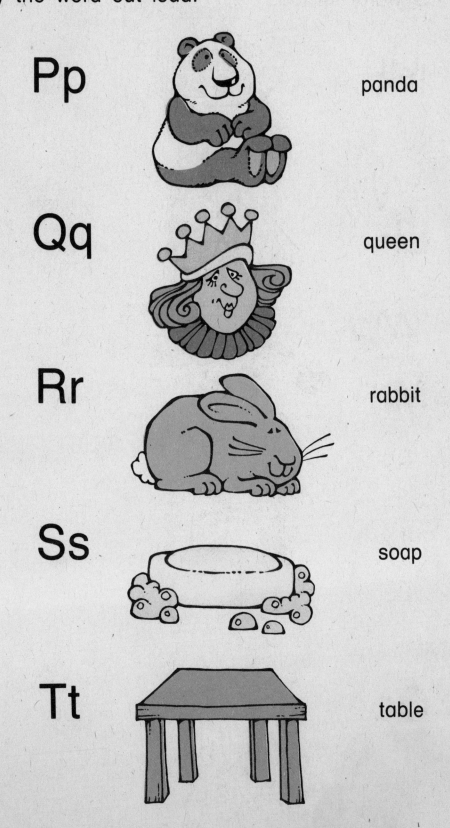

Pp   panda

Qq   queen

Rr   rabbit

Ss   soap

Tt   table

Say the name
of the letter.
Then say the word out loud.

Uu  urn

Vv 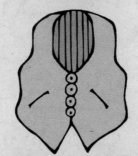 vest

Ww  wagon

Xx  x-ray

Yy  yo-yo

Zz  zebra

Some letters make good sounds.
Say the sounds out loud.

Color the picture.

26

In each line
put an X on the picture
that does not belong.

hot dog	hot dog	hot dog	cold drink
ice cream	ice cream	peanuts	ice cream
cold drink	cold drink	cold drink	hot pretzel
peanuts	hot dog	peanuts	peanuts
ice cream	hot pretzel	hot pretzel	hot pretzel

Draw a line from the words
to the picture.

hot pretzel

hot dog

cold drink

ice cream

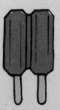

peanuts

28

Read the words.
Say them out loud.

hot

hot dog

hot pretzel

pretzel

dog

ice cream

cold drink

drink

peanuts

Read the words.
Color the picture.

SHOES BAKERY SPORTS

Read the words
in the window.
Say them out loud.

SANDALS

LOAFERS

SNEAKERS

BOOTS

SADDLE
SHOES

SLIPPERS

32

Read the words
in the window.
Say them out loud.

Read the words
in the window.
Say them out loud.

Read the words
in the window.
Say them out loud.

Read the words
in the window.
Say them out loud.

Read the words
in the window.
Say them out loud.

This boy got one thing
in each store.
Color the picture.

In each line
put an X on the picture
that does not belong.

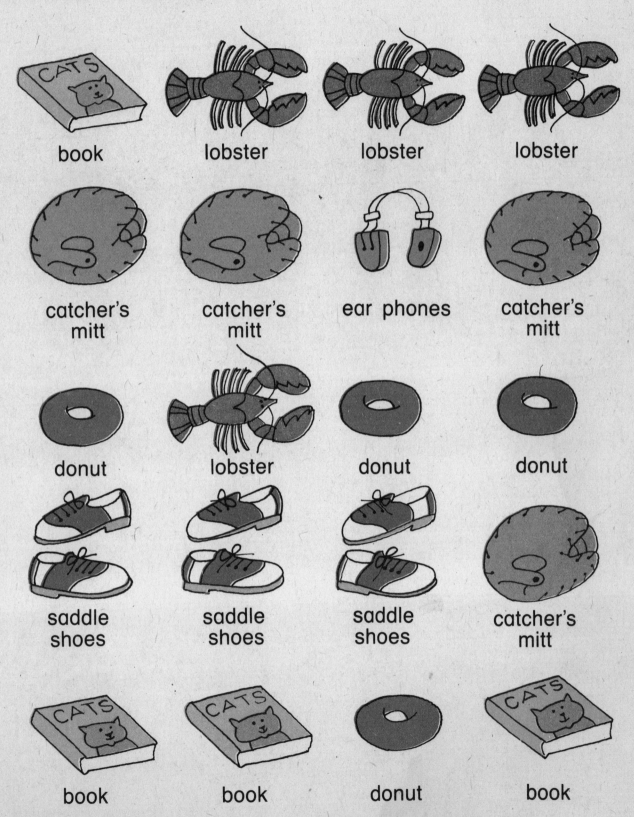

book   lobster   lobster   lobster

catcher's   catcher's   ear phones   catcher's
mitt   mitt   mitt

donut   lobster   donut   donut

saddle   saddle   saddle   catcher's
shoes   shoes   shoes   mitt

book   book   donut   book

Draw a line from the words
to the picture.

ear phones

donut

catcher's mitt

book

saddle shoes

lobster

Read the words.
Say them out loud.

ear phones

ear

donut

saddle shoes

catcher's mitt

mitt

lobster

Read the words out loud.

cookies

TV

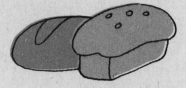

bread

boots

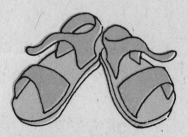

sandals

ball

story book

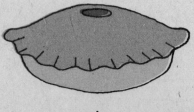

pie

sneakers

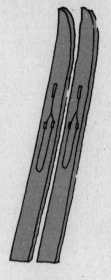

skis

clams

cake

skates

television

slippers

book

Words for People

Color the people.

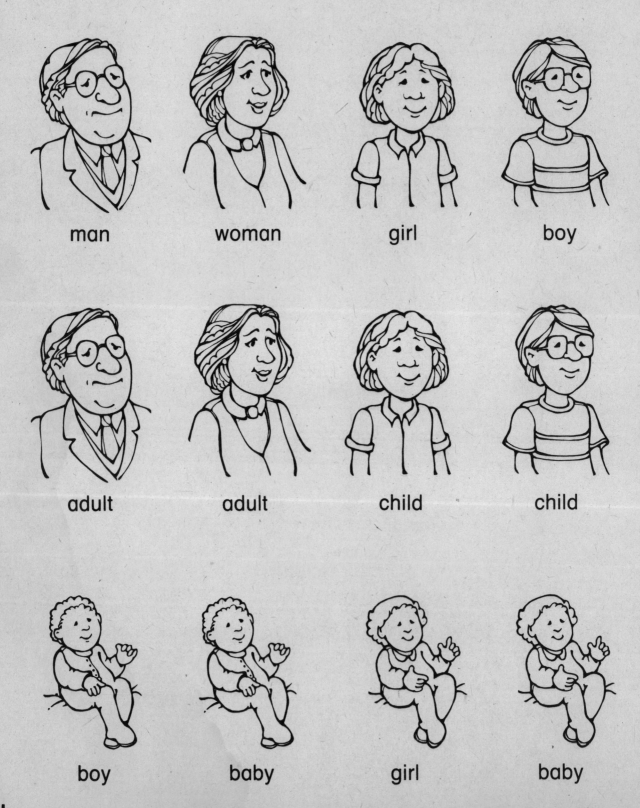

man   woman   girl   boy

adult   adult   child   child

boy   baby   girl   baby

In each line
put an X on the picture
that does not belong.

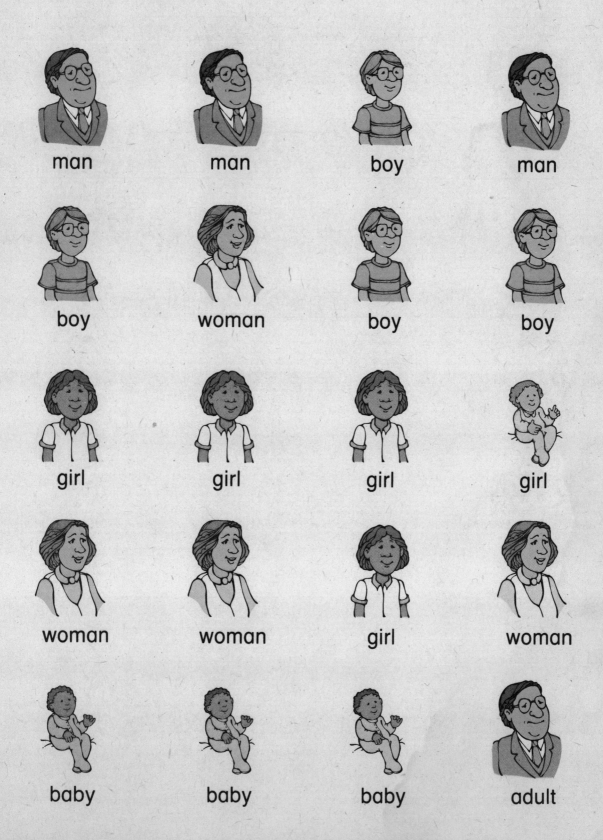

man	man	boy	man
boy	woman	boy	boy
girl	girl	girl	girl
woman	woman	girl	woman
baby	baby	baby	adult

Draw a line between the pictures
that are exactly the same.

man

boy

woman

man

girl

girl

boy

girl

girl

boy

boy

woman

Draw a line between the pictures that are exactly the same.

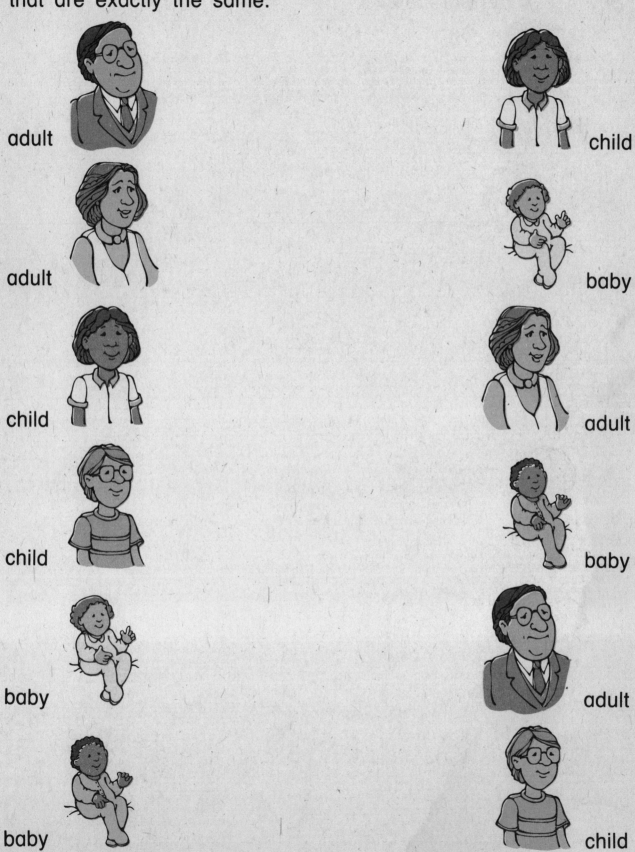

adult

adult

child

child

baby

baby

child

baby

adult

baby

adult

child

Words about Families

Say the words out loud.
Color the pictures.

brother   sister

mother

father

grandmother   grandfather

aunt   uncle

daughter   son

Words for Places

Say the words out loud.

Draw a line from the words
to the picture.

post office

theater

stadium

zoo

More Words for Places

Say the words out loud.

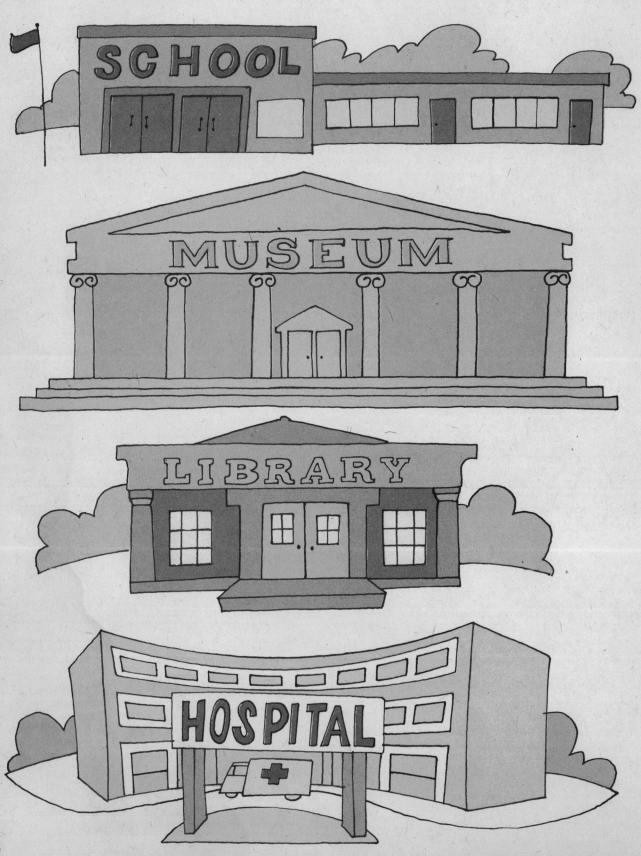

Draw a line from the word
to the picture.

school

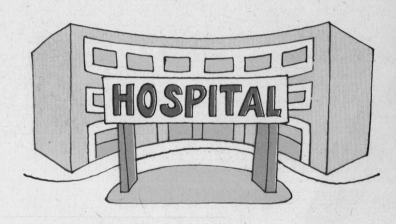

museum

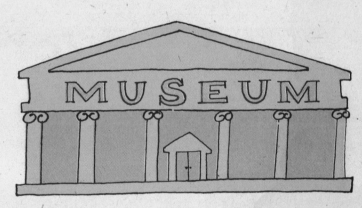

library

hospital

Words for Clothes

Say the words out loud.

shirt

pants

shoes

socks

skirt

dress

sweater

coat

cap

boots

jacket

slicker

In each line
put an X on the picture
that does not belong.

shoes   shoes   socks   shoes

socks   boots   socks   socks

coat   cap   cap   cap

shirt   shirt   skirt   shirt

coat   coat   coat   dress

Color the picture.

Ss

Say these words out loud.

snake   sing   sneeze

soup   sit   stop

Ww

Say these words out loud.

window   wheel   weed

whistle   water

A parade is fun.
Watching is fun.
Reading is fun too.
Find all the words in the picture.

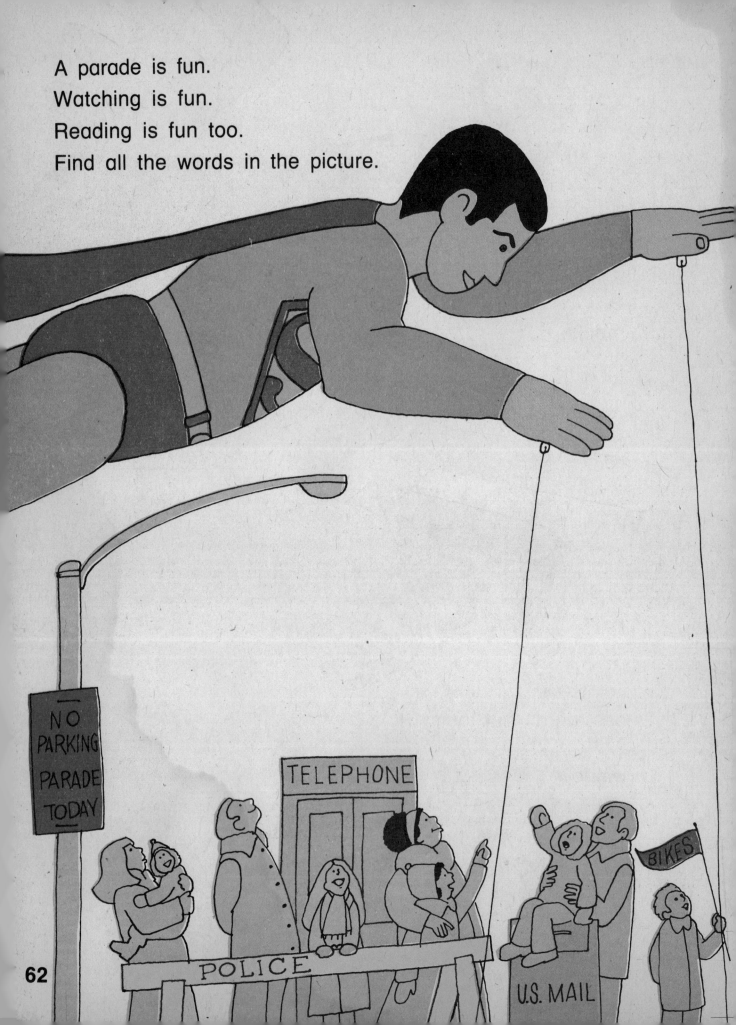

NO PARKING PARADE TODAY

TELEPHONE

BIKES

POLICE

U.S. MAIL

63